Teacher's

By Nancy Prasad
Illustrated by Joan Holub

Pet Show
Today!

Houghton Mifflin Company Boston

Atlanta   Dallas   Geneva, Illinois   Palo Alto   Princeton

Rose brings her rabbit.

Cathy brings her cat.

Wayne brings his hamster.

Bobby brings his rat.

Tam brings her turtle.

David brings his dog.

Carla brings her caterpillar.

Fred brings his frog.

"It looks like a zoo in here,"
says Mrs. Ruiz with a smile.

"Wait and see who I've brought in for just a little while!"